feathers	moon	reeds	tail
feet	nest	sail	tears
leaf	pig	stye	twig
Morris Mouse	pond	sunshine	water
Mummy Duck	puddle	swim	waterfall

Every morning  took her  for a  in the  .

One by one they dived into the  . Then, they each wiggled a little  before playing happily in the  .

When 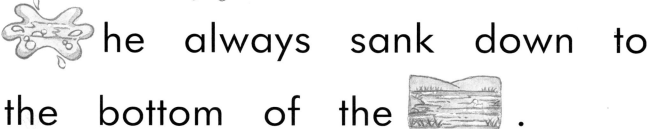 dived into the he always sank down to the bottom of the .

Poor ! He just could not learn how to . All the other laughed at him.

"Surely all can !" quacked crossly.

"Not all! " mumbled . Her  was full of Dally's , which she was holding up out of the  . The rest of him had sunk. She got very tired trying to teach to . Soon hid amongst the when the other went swimming. He was very lonely

One day, (mouse) was walking happily along when he found (duck) with (tears) (tears) in his (eyes) .

"What is the matter?" asked (mouse) . Then, poor (duck) told how the other (ducks) had all made fun of him for not swimming. (mouse) felt sorry for (duck) . "Come and be my friend," he said. Together, (mouse) and (duck) set off to explore the (farm) .

They called on Percy  at his home in his  .

"Please," (mouse) asked politely, "do you know why (duck) is not able to (swim) ?"

"I heard about a (pig) who could fly," grunted Percy, "but never a duck who could not (swim). Ask Buttercup (cow) . She might know the answer."

(mouse) and (duck) went to the meadow where Buttercup and all the (cows) lived.

"Poor ," moo-ed Buttercup when they asked her how could learn to .

"There was once a who jumped over the 🌙 but I have

never heard of a duck who
could not . Why not
practise in a nice big ?"
 found a big deep
and  waded straight in.

At first,  looked as if
he was really swimming

But, he still had his
on the bottom. sank when
he tried to lift them up.

Just then, saw an old
 floating by, coming towards
them. We'll build a ," he
cried. "Then we can both float
on the  ."

Together they pulled the
from the  and carried
it down to the  .

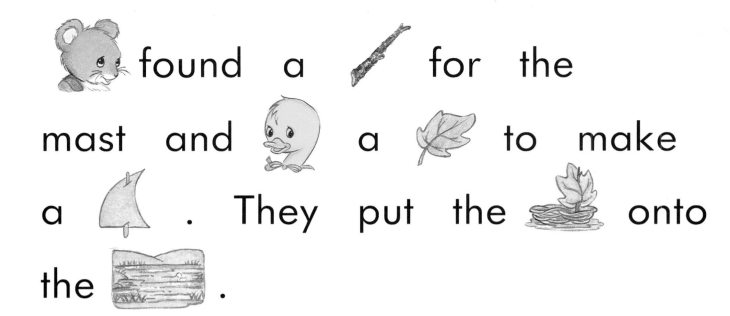 found a ⟋ for the mast and 🐤 a 🍃 to make a ⛵ . They put the 🍂 onto the ▨ .

It floated so beautifully that 🐤 and 🐭 climbed aboard.

Happily, the two friends sailed off into the ☀ .

Around the ▨ they drifted and onto the little stream that ran between the 🌿 .

 and were having so much fun that they did not notice how fast the little was moving along.

On and on sped the .

Suddenly, with a whoosh and a splash, the  sailed over a small  and broke into pieces. The two friends were thrown into the  .

"Help! Help!" cried .

"I cannot . I'm sinking!"

Poor 🐤 kicked his 👟 and wriggled his 〰️ with all his might to try and keep himself afloat. Then, to his surprise, 🐤 found he had reached his friend 🐭 and was pulling him to safety.

"You swam! You really swam!" cried 🐭 as 🐤 got his breath back. Nobody was more surprised than 🐤 .

It was a long and cold walk home to the and it was dark by the time and his friend arrived. dried Dally's and was really pleased to see him and safely home.

Now, goes with all the every day for a . Sometimes goes too, riding on his friend's back.